BOARDS:

Purposes,
Organizations,
Procedures

BOARDS:
Purposes,
Organizations,
Procedures

A Practical Guide to
Effective Boards

Tilman R. Smith

HERALD PRESS
Scottdale, Pennsylvania
Kitchener, Ontario
1978

BOARDS: Purposes, Organizations, Procedures
Copyright © 1978 by Herald Press, Scottdale, Pa. 15683
    Published simultaneously in Canada by Herald Press,
    Kitchener, Ont. N2G 4M5
Library of Congress Catalog Card Number: 78-62628
International Standard Book Number: 0-8361-1862-6
Printed in the United States of America
Design: Alice B. Shetler

10 9 8 7 6 5 4 3 2 1

Contents

Notes secular as in religious organizations. Operating boards of either secular or religious organizations will find the material in this book readily adaptable to their specific circumstances.

The procedures outlined on the pages that follow are not intended as immutable laws. This guide is meant to supplement, not supplant, present board procedures. Space is provided for notes.

If these guidelines help your board sharpen up its procedures or broaden its perspective of its total task, then I am confident you will derive equal satisfaction from the methods of decision making as from the decision itself.

Tilman R. Smith
Goshen, Indiana

10

Author's Preface

The material in this book is presented from a practical rather than a theoretical background. It is based on information gathered as an administrator, as a member of various boards, and from experiences as a consultant. There are few footnotes and quotes.

My administrative experience covers twenty-five years as a public school superintendent, two years as vice-president of a manufacturing company, and nine years in college administration. I have served on the boards of many community, state, and church agencies.

Legitimate and appropriate areas in which individual boards must feel responsible cannot be defined precisely. In boards with which I have been associated the following rule of thumb based on the division of powers by the Canadian and U.S. governments has been helpful: powers not enumerated or implied specifically for the federal governments are residual or "leftover" powers for the provinces or states. Accordingly boards should:

(1) Be very careful that their actions do not supersede or infringe upon the prerogatives, directives, or authority of any organized body to whom they are responsible which outranks them.

(2) Accept as their responsibility all appropriate and necessary functions and duties which are not designated for some other body. Generally these residual powers cover a wide range and need sharp scrutiny. It is just as hazardous for boards to fail to understand their full mandates as it is to infringe upon the rights of other agencies.

My practical involvement in church organizations was enhanced by ten years or more in each of the following churchwide boards: Mennonite Mutual Aid, Mennonite Board of Missions Health and Welfare Committee, Mennonite Board of Education, and the Schowalter Foundation.

The suggestions of many persons have been incorporated into this book. Two or more members of each of the Mennonite churchwide boards kindly critiqued the manuscript. Several organizational consultants gave solid proposals, and an attorney added his blessing to these ideas.

The request for writing this booklet came from the Health and Welfare Committee of Mennonite Board of Missions, Elkhart, Indiana. I sincerely thank all those whose interest and generous help made this volume possible.

Although some of the illustrations have their background in religious organizations, much of the material grows out of experience in nonchurch organizations, including public school boards.

Good decisions, I believe, arise from consensus. Consensus methods are just as important and potentially effective in

duties which are not designated for some other body. Generally these residual powers cover a wide range and need sharp scrutiny. It is just as hazardous for boards to fail to understand their full mandates as it is to infringe upon the rights of other agencies.

My practical involvement in church organizations was enhanced by ten years or more in each of the following churchwide boards: Mennonite Mutual Aid, Mennonite Board of Missions Health and Welfare Committee, Mennonite Board of Education, and the Schowalter Foundation.

The suggestions of many persons have been incorporated into this book. Two or more members of each of the Mennonite churchwide boards kindly critiqued the manuscript. Several organizational consultants gave solid proposals, and an attorney added his blessing to these ideas.

The request for writing this booklet came from the Health and Welfare Committee of Mennonite Board of Missions, Elkhart, Indiana. I sincerely thank all those whose interest and generous help made this volume possible.

Although some of the illustrations have their background in religious organizations, much of the material grows out of experience in nonchurch organizations, including public school boards.

Good decisions, I believe, arise from consensus. Consensus methods are just as important and potentially effective in secular as in religious organizations. Operating boards of either secular or religious organizations will find the material in this book readily adaptable to their specific circumstances.

The procedures outlined on the pages that follow are not intended as immutable laws. This guide is meant to supplement, not supplant, present board procedures. Space is provided for notes.

If these guidelines help your board sharpen up its procedures or broaden its perspective of its total task, then I am confident you will derive equal satisfaction from the methods of decision making as from the decision itself.

Tilman R. Smith
Goshen, Indiana

Introduction

Organized groups and societies have generally delegated authority and responsibility to smaller bodies for managerial and supervisory purposes. Persons making up these smaller bodies have various names such as board-members, commissioners, trustees, directors, overseers, managers, and so on. In this study the term BOARD will be used to cover all titles used for such managerial and supervisory groups.

In some organizations a committee may be delegated the same responsibilities as boards in others. In this study, however, COMMITTEE will refer to a small group authorized to investigate, to take action on specific delegated duties, and to report back to the board—but not to manage or supervise in a general way.

Operating boards of various kinds are a North American phenomenon. It is also typically North American to assume that almost any problem can be solved by the appointment of a committee. We humorously remark that of the making of committees there is no end. It is my personal conclusion and affirmation based on more than forty years of administrative experience in educational, business, church, and community agencies that board members, serving on a voluntary basis, bring a quality of service to our institutions that money could not buy.

11

I think of one newly organized, unified school district in which I served as superintendent. The board met fifty-one times during the first year. One member, a farmer, drove more than 1,000 miles to attend meetings that year entirely at his own expense.

I have seldom, if ever, felt that any member on the boards of the institutions with which I was associated served for a selfish purpose. I salute the North American system of operating institutions with persons chosen from the broader constituency or from the community who serve without remuneration at great personal sacrifice but with real commitment and common sense.

Committees have been a great service also, especially if they are appointed for specific tasks with proper terminal arrangements, free from ceremonial or prestige motivations. Volunteerism in North America is making many unique contributions to community and church life.

Organizing the Board

1. Choosing board members

There probably is no single best method for electing or selecting persons to serve on boards. Most organizations stipulate the methods in their constitutions or bylaws. Regardless of the method, we cannot be too careful in evaluating the gifts of the persons we are calling to serve on our boards. It is extremely important that all board members recognize the fact that they are to serve a constituency directly or indirectly, and that the wishes of the constituency must always be held in highest priority.

Processes which permit boards to be self-perpetuating should be sharply questioned and probably changed. A constituency should never be divested of full recourse in selecting, directing, and holding accountable, its agents. The process for terminating board memberships must be carefully outlined and exercised with integrity.

2. Board size

A board should be of sufficient size that the gifts needed for its purposes will be represented, but not so large that each member doesn't feel a vital, personal obligation for involvement.

A board may be too large if members feel that it is insignificant if they miss meetings for other than emergency rea-   **13** sons, and it may be too small if members feel too much personal responsibility.

Depending on the type of organization, five to eleven members should represent a workable combination.

II.

Qualifications for Board Members
3. General considerations

• Board members should be dynamic persons with a high degree of integrity and a good sense of justice.

• They should be objective, willing to look at all sides of a question before making decisions.

• They should be willing to serve, to learn, to be good listeners, good performers, sound decision-makers.

• They should have the ability to conceptualize; that is, to visualize outcomes.

• They should understand their roles as board members.

• They should be futuristic in outlook but also have an understanding and respect for the past.

• Educational background is not the highest priority; board members are not expected to be professionals. Boards hire professionals for the internal jobs. However, formal educational achievement or certain types of experience may be helpful.

• There must be a proper mix of board members, of sufficient tenure and continuity and adequate managerial ability

"We both want to do the Lord's will, you in your way and I in His."

14

to head the total enterprise. A proper mix should include women, men, and minority groups which make up a constituency. The board does not manage directly the internal affairs but it is legally and ethically vested with responsibility for the total enterprise. The effectiveness of boards generally rises or falls on the basis of the administrator they are able to hire and to hold, and the kind of professional staff which the administrator can attract. The policies of the board must be such that competency can be rewarded and the full gifts of all personnel utilized.

• Board members should be able to distinguish between the affairs which they should manage directly and the affairs which are to be duly delegated to the administrator and the staff.

4. Check your motivation

Persons asked to serve on boards or who allow themselves to become candidates for election, should:

• Honestly and objectively answer such questions as:

   (a) Am I willing to take the time to become knowledgeable in the area?

   (b) Can I develop enthusiasm for the job?

   (c) Am I willing to attend all meetings and participate positively in decisions?

   (d) Am I willing to promote the general cause outside of meetings?

• Sort through hidden agendas to

check out conflicts of interest which may arise. The late Walter Lippmann observed that "public opinion is not necessarily based on what is true but on what people think is true."

• Avoid serving on primary boards or committees when you already serve on another board or committee directly responsible to the same parent organization. It is difficult to be objective when serving on several boards with competing purposes, interests, or functions. Generally, an organized body has sufficient personnel resources available so that dual memberships or overlapping are neither necessary nor desirable.

III.

Orientation

5. For the board member

New board members need to be made aware of purposes, procedures, expectations, and background information regarding their responsibilities. Generally, the administrator with the cooperation of the board chairperson supplies such information and outlines the procedures which have been commonly followed. The chairperson needs to sharpen up the goals and purposes along with expectations which have in the past been found to be helpful and significant. Other continuing board members should share their experiences.

16   Administrators, as continuing persons

whose tenure often covers the terms of different members, should supply orientation materials which will help new members find their way to effective membership on the board as soon as possible.

Effective board membership is a learning process which takes time to develop. However, new members should not shrink from sharing their opinions as they learn. No member ever learns all there is to know, so in a real sense experience is a relative term.

Newly selected board members, as a part of their orientation, should learn the specific purposes, the general intentions, and the expectations of the constituency which selects them. New members must be given adequate background information regarding procedures, responsibilities, and understandings, many of which may not be in writing.

6. For the administrator

New administrators also need orientation. The board and the staff have obligations for orienting administrators seeking out information about procedures. Administrators may not be able to absorb all the counsel given, but they should listen carefully and make judgments only after weighing all the information which has been received.

Administrators need to remind themselves that they never learn to know all there is to know either! 17

IV.

To Whom Is the Board Responsible?

7. General understandings

It is extremely important that boards understand their relationship to other boards, the constituencies they serve, and the line of authority above and below. Some boards do not serve a constituency directly but are part of a structure with lines and layers of authority. This can become complicated.

It is difficult to outline the exact steps through the maze of intricate relationships which exist between various boards, committees, and personnel in the church and community. Considering questions such as these may help:

• How can good understandings be established and maintained?

• How can we identify and resolve "gray areas"?

• How can good decisions be made?

• How can we be sensitive to one another's rights and respect each other?

8. Authority vested in appointments

The authority vested in appointment of board members symbolizes the line of responsibility. Every board should find out to whom it is directly responsible, whether it be to another board, to a specific constituency, to a governmental agency, or to a general church or community body and by what authority and power it was appointed.

18   Institutional boards should regularly

make written reports to the agency to which they are directly responsible and to the body of ultimate responsibility if not the same agency.

9. Responsibility—some special cases

Some boards have been established on an *ad hoc* basis without determining fully to whom they were responsible. A board selected by patrons of a private school, for instance, may seek wider church support without being responsible to the supporting group.

In another instance, a corporation is formed which operates a private school and the corporation selects the board. The corporation has minimal responsibility to local congregations and to the conference in general.

Some private elementary school boards are selected by only one congregation, although the patrons are from a broader area. The financial support and patronage from the broader constituency in such a case comes without representation.

A retirement home was organized many years ago by a group of patrons with a self-perpetuating board. It has now outgrown its organizational structure and also its facilities. Now it has no broad constituency to fall back upon for the support it needs.

These kinds of relationships should be carefully reexamined. If we claim to be church sponsored organizations and expect support from congregations, financial or otherwise, we must be sure they are represented on our boards.

V.

Suggestions for Board Members and Administrators

10. The role and responsibilities of the board

• The board should first determine its goals, philosophy, objectives, and purposes and keep them under constant review.

• Its next most important role is to select an able administrator who in turn recommends the best possible professional and nonprofessional staff.

• In addition to selecting and maintaining a qualified staff, and generally as a condition thereof, effective communication must be developed and maintained throughout the whole system. This is tremendously important because people cannot do their best when they are not heard, understood, and supported in their problems and in the best exercise of their gifts. The need for clear understanding cannot be overemphasized. It is often the so-called little things which cause stress and distress. These conditions are not new; King Solomon wrote, "Catch us the foxes, the little foxes, that spoil the vineyards" (Song of Solomon 2:15, RSV).

• The board must delegate authority but it cannot delegate ultimate responsibility.

• It must determine with the cooperation of all groups directly involved, the scope of services to be offered.

• It must plan for delivering these services most effectively and efficiently. Planning is an ongoing activity and never ends. There should be short-range and long-range plans, all consistent with the objectives.

• The board has external responsibility for the total climate of the institution, assuring conditions in which all can work efficiently toward one common end—the best services for all.

• It is a continuing legal agency whose ultimate authority comes from the constituency. It has final responsibility for finances, planned expansion, maintenance, accreditation, major policy decisions, the general programs, and allied activities. It is legally and morally responsible for all policies which are set.

• The board is not made up of persons who serve as professionals. It must, therefore, solicit and expect a continuous flow of creative input from the administrator. The administrator in turn must involve the professional staff and the constituency in gathering the best thinking of all concerned, making suggestions and recommendations to the board, particularly about internal affairs.

• The board needs to analyze and evaluate solid information from the administration, staff, and constituents in the form of verbal and written reports and studies.

21

• It should frequently review objectives, restudy purposes, inquire about deficiencies, correct deviations from sound procedures, and constantly analyze performance so there is no comfortable tendency to do things routinely. It can effectively accomplish this task by asking the significant questions. This is one of the board members' most important responsibilities. Learn to ask the right questions. Board members are expected to be generalists and not specialists in the enterprise they supervise. They should expect the true status of the daily operating program to come from the administrator. Unless questioned sharply, some administrators may be too selective in the information they choose to disclose. They should be pushed for solid answers and substantive supporting data. Easy questions and glib answers will not tell board members what they ought to know; they may even be deluded and unwarily led astray by inadequate information. Asking the right question is really a vote of confidence in good administration.

• The board is a final court of appeals for anyone in the institution. A request to come before the board, however, must follow a proper procedure previously outlined.

• It is responsible to interpret the institution to the community it serves and to enlist the cooperation of all segments of its constituency.

22 • It must establish sound procedures

for doing business efficiently and for the implementation of board decisions.

11. The administrator as executive officer

Administrators are the chief executive officers of boards and also chief representatives of the total staff to the board when it is in session. They are the professional leaders. They set the tone internally and to a great extent determine the quality of the program. The administrator's highest responsibility is to attract, recruit, and hold good persons and then set up conditions whereby employees can do a good job. The administrator must assist the board in establishing and implementing such general policies and procedures which become effective tools in the process, rather than binding the institution into a straightjacket.

After the board has developed the overall policies, it is the duty of the administrator to implement these policies on a day-to-day basis. Administrators must make decisions for the board between board sessions which are within the province of delegated authority and which are in line with board policies and principles.

It is the administrator's duty to keep the board well informed between meetings of what is happening that would be of special interest and which might help them answer questions which may arise in the community. Such information often prevents embarrassment for board members.

23

The administrator must make broad contacts with the constituency to keep it informed of the significant activities which are taking place in the institution, to interpret both board actions and institutional functions to the community, and to enlist their understanding and support.

12. The administrator's relationship to staff

The administrator must develop clear and concise internal procedures in which all know what they are supposed to do.

For the board, for the administrator, and for all concerned the most important job is to recruit good personnel. The administrator should enlist the cooperation of the staff in filling positions. Recruitment is a vigorous enterprise and good prospects should be explored even though candidates may be numerous. Sources of personnel should be carefully checked and recommendations solicited from a wide variety of sources. It is good to have candidates visit the institution and become acquainted with other personnel there and with the procedures involved.

Orientation of personnel is very important and doesn't end with a few initial lessons. It is a continuous process. The obligation to help staff persons do their best is one which never ends. Sometimes it is an advantage to ask an experienced person to help a new employee in certain

24

areas. However, administrators can never abandon their responsibility to any staff person.

The administrator with the board should provide for a redress of grievances. Persons who have concerns should know there is a proper procedure for stating their cases.

Administrators should be futuristic in outlook but also realistic. They should seriously ponder, "Where do we want this institution to be next year? in five years? in ten years? How are we going to get there?" Administrators and boards should enlist the cooperation of the whole community in seeking answers to these questions.

Administrators stand between the public, as represented by the board, and the staff. They must be able to support staff through understanding what they are assigned to do.

The administrator and the staff must relate the institution to the needs of the community or constituency it exists to serve.

VI.

The "Four F" Policy
13. For all involved.
- Be frank.
- Be fair.
- Be firm.
- Be friendly.

25

VII.

Caution
14. To board members

Make sure you know which powers are to be duly delegated and which are to be directly retained—which ones are policy-making and which of the powers are administrative.

Often, persons who serve on boards have not served at that level before. They may have gained experience through serving on committees, but those relationships and functions are different. Usually, a committee is directly responsible to a board and not to a constituency. A committee has a specific assignment, and is not an ongoing entity. Generally, it has a small membership and its procedures can be less formal.

Persons who become members of boards must be oriented to understand the differences between boards and committees. Board members should realize that a more formal procedure is necessary because the decisions of a board, which may include committee recommendations, carry a responsibility directly to a constituency.

15. To administrators

The legal body is the board; its function is legislative. If administrators dominate discussions with too many fixed opinions and suggestions, board members may become intimidated and disinterested.

The chairperson of the board must be in control of the meeting; the administrator's job is to furnish information, suggest different options, make recommendations when asked, and to understand fully the implications of the board's contemplated actions. Strong administrators seek to understand their roles and are able to conceptualize their duties both in board sessions and between sessions.

VIII.

The Board in Operation

16. Adjust procedures to the type of meeting

The chairperson may be called on to chair two kinds of meetings—regular board meetings and general meetings of the constituency to which the board is responsible. Some of the procedures suggested would not be appropriate for every kind of meeting and on every occasion. For instance, for regular small board meetings not every suggestion listed on the following pages would need to be followed. However, the principles are correct and their purposes are valid.

It is important in small groups as it is in large ones to protect the rights of each individual. This can be done more informally in small groups.

17. Principles underlying proper procedures

Good procedures do not emerge 27

simply because an organization is made up of Christians serving a Christian constituency. Ignorance can separate persons from their reasonable rights as effectively as can duplicity.

Some are frightened by the suggestion of parliamentary procedures. Instead, they suggest consensus. They do not realize that to develop consensus effectively proper parliamentary procedures must be used. True consensus does not emerge from a haphazard, unguided approach but is subject to some well-defined and carefully directed procedures. The aim of good parliamentary procedure is to give every person involved the right to help in making good decisions which can be positively supported by a large majority, by everyone who is involved if possible.

Second, a reasonable knowledge of proper procedure is necessary for a meeting to run smoothly and for chairpersons to carry out their duties well. A meeting should not be disrupted because technical points are raised legitimately and no one seems to know how to proceed.

In the third place, some meetings have been thrown into confusion for frivolous or obstructing reasons. Every chairperson should master a basic knowledge of parliamentary procedure, but in special cases the chairperson may call upon someone better versed in parliamentary procedure than himself to correct a chaotic proceeding.

Some principles for conducting business in organized meetings follow.[1]

(a) Rules and regulations help facilitate the transaction of business and promote cooperation and harmony.

(b) The vote of the majority decides and whenever a person joins a group he tacitly agrees to be governed by majority decisions. As often as possible the majority vote should represent the will of all—a consensus.

(c) Every member has equal rights, privileges, and obligations.

(d) Minorities have rights which must be protected.

(e) Full and free discussion on every proposition presented for decision is an established right for each.

(f) The simplest and most direct procedures for accomplishing a purpose should be followed. Everyone should be able to understand and, as far as possible, technicalities should be avoided. Correct procedures should not be considered technicalities, however.

(g) Motions have a definite and logical procedural order. After a motion has been made and supported it can be amended and the amendment can be amended. However, even at this stage there are other motions which have precedence over the above motions in this order:

---

1. General ideas are from Alice F. Sturgis, *Standard Code of Parliamentary Procedure,"* McGraw-Hill Book Company, New York, 1966.

- *To adjourn.*
- *To recess until a specific time.*
- *To raise a question of privilege.* Example: a member may find it necessary to leave, for which a reason is given.
- *To lay the motion on the table.*
- *To raise a point of order.* (While these procedures are authentic, and a chairperson should be acquainted with them, for regular board sessions they may be too technical. For instance, if a motion needs serious revision calling for amendments, it may be better to start with a new motion.)

(h) Every member has a right to know at all times the question before the body and what its purpose is. If a member should say, "I move the previous question," all members should know that if they approve voting on the "previous question," this means debate is shut off.

(i) Only one question can be considered at a time, although the first motion may be superseded by a motion of higher precedence (see g).

(j) Those to whom power is delegated must be chosen by a democratic process. Self-perpetuating boards or self-appointed officers cannot be trusted or expected to be vigilant concerning the rights of others.

(k) Presiding officers must be strictly impartial. In order to be impartial they must understand and apply proper procedures. Generally they should not be-

30

come involved in controversies. If, as a presiding officer, one feels that it is essential to argue a certain point, this should be done, but sparingly and judiciously. In chairing larger groups it might be better for the chairperson to ask another person to preside.

18. The agenda

The development and implementation of the agenda are extremely important. Who is responsible?

In general, most of the agenda items will emerge from the day-to-day experiences of the administrator who should keep a special file folder for agenda items as they arise. Before the board session, the chairperson should confer with the administrator and add items which he or she might have. Other board members should be invited also to suggest items. The tentative agenda should then be made available to all board members before the board sessions, for study.

In submitting the tentative agenda to all members, the administrator may also report on how directives from previous meetings were carried out and give other information board members should have. Providing advance background information for agenda items will save time at board sessions.

When the board is in session, the agenda should be reviewed and provisions made for the addition of other items.

Seldom is there time for full consideration of all items. As the agenda is reviewed, the items should be classified into priorities and a decision made as to which items should be considered first, which are less pressing, and which may be held for a later meeting.

Some general consideration should also be given on how much time to allot to each of the items selected for consideration. Since the board has limited time to give to each item, a time schedule for the selected items should be blocked out. The purpose of this is not to thwart full discussion but rather to make every member conscious of keeping discussions germane and to make certain that all the items to be considered are given a fair share of time. Extraneous comments might be interesting but may not add to understanding.

The implementation of the agenda is the responsibility of the chairperson, but there must be good coordination and understanding with the administrator. Too often, urgent items which may not be the most pertinent get too much time and tend to crowd out more important ones.

19. Integrity in board decisions

To make authentic decisions, board members must have data in sufficient detail and in adequate time to process the material. If board members have to make decisions without sufficient data and time to understand, they are "de facto" and not boards in the real sense they were meant to be. It is the responsibility in most cases for administrators to furnish the raw material on which to base the decisions.

At times administrators carry procedures between board sessions beyond the point of no return. Boards are then virtually forced to ratify decisions already made. When boards lose complete freedom of choice, although their decisions are still binding, they are mechanical and may not represent real board thinking.

Strong administrators with true leadership qualities do not push boards into positions in which members may have to surrender their rights to make free decisions with integrity. Procedures for handling emergency situations should be provided in prior plans. However, if too many "emergency" situations arise, the board should examine its administrator's leadership.

20. Working toward consensus

In regular board sessions it is important that all members can come to support the ultimate decision. It takes adequate data, time for understanding, and the interaction of each person to come to a meeting of the minds on each issue. However, it is my experience that this can be done. At times, it may require a postponement of a decision until better information is available, and possibly some changes in approach—a compro-

The school superintendent got a get well card in the hospital from his board. It said, "Sent to you by official action of the board 4 to 3."

mise on details without compromising principles.

In debating issues in which we are honestly seeking for points of agreement and consensus we must be careful not to become unduly defensive of a point of view, nor can we afford to push members beyond their honest convictions. There should be no stigma attached to disagreeing agreeably.

A primary objective of every board should be to arrive at viable decisions through consensus. Consensus is a judgment arrived at by a substantial majority of those directly concerned. It is often, although not always, a unanimous decision reflecting the true sense of the meeting. Groups which uphold this method of decision making assume in principle that as individual members they will give support to the common judgments arrived at through proper methods by a substantial majority of those concerned, even though not every detail might be personally endorsed. Decisions in which less than 80 or 90 percent of those involved agree are questionable.

Attaining consensus is practical in secular organizations as well as in religious bodies. Developing consensus may not always seem like an efficient use of time as contrasted with more arbitrary methods. Consensus takes time, understanding, proper procedures, adequate information, and respect for each individual opinion on the part of boards and administrators. Moreover, the methods used in coming to a decision are sometimes just as important as the ultimate decision. A proper decision arrived at improperly leaves doubts and trampled feelings. It leads to a loss of support in implementing decisions.

21. What does consensus mean?

Consensus means that board members or other groups are ready to give their general consent and approval to an action after carefully reasoning together. It implies that the body believes that the proposed action finally hammered out represents the best collective opinion that can be expected on that issue at that particular time and situation. Unity is attained but there may not be complete unanimity. There is harmony in accepting some compromise of individual opinion on certain details, a willingness to set aside some personal preferences.

Consensus may be more closely identified with method than with final decision. The ideal is to use processes in decision making whereby each person involved feels that the technique used for coming to a conclusion was open and fair, each had a chance to be heard, that all proper resources were used, ample information was available, there were no hidden agendas, and there was no attempt at coercion or embarrassment.

Consensus should be tested at various steps in the discussion by giving opportunity for every participant to ask 35 further questions and to express reservations or affirmations about what seems to be emerging as the general sense of the meeting on the particular question at issue. The chairperson should see that accommodation is made for covering as many suggestions or reservations as possible which do not distort the general intent of the main action under consideration.

Not every action needs to be recorded by a formal vote. However, when a consensus is reached the chairperson should declare that a consensus seems to have been reached, and if there are no objections or further suggestions, the secretary shall be instructed to state in the minutes that a general consensus on that question has been reached and the action so recorded.

22. Voting

Although decisions should ultimately spring from general consensus, this does not mean that a vote should be omitted. When the chairperson feels that there is a general meeting of the minds on an issue, a vote should be called for: voice, show of hands, or ballot. Testing by voting is generally a fairer method of determining consensus than for the chairperson to arbitrarily announce that there is consensus. The vote records the consensus. In some organizations (some school boards for instance), it is legally required that each member's vote be individually recorded. Other organizational bylaws require that the general vote be recorded.

23. Present but not voting

There are times when members cannot individually come to a comfortable conclusion, and decide not to vote. When a member is present but not voting or simply votes "present," that member is agreeing to go along with the majority.

24. Voting negatively

No organization can function effectively unless there is general agreement on basic issues. Frequent badly divided votes tend to fracture relationships and may indicate that the administrator and board members have not done their homework as carefully as they should have. Split votes also encourage the constituency to become confused in trying to determine which side was right.

The administrator should not bring recommendations until they are carefully researched and found viable. Board members should not be asked to make a decision until they feel a consensus to act positively, or to ask for further information before making a decision.

There may be circumstances when it is necessary to make a decision at a given time and a divided vote results. Persons of integrity and goodwill cannot always agree. It is much better to vote one's convictions than to move along with something which we may feel is wrong. These cases should be rare, however, and if there is frequent recurrence, the methods of decision making should be examined.

25. Limitations of consensus

Obviously in operating institutions administrators cannot call everyone together every time a decision has to be made. However, administrators should make their decisions with input from those who are directly responsible for the implementation of decisions. Anyone involved in the decision should have the freedom to come to the administrator with suggestions for improvements in methods or for better understanding.

Since administrators are directly responsible to operating boards for the implementation of policy already established, their directives depend more on good communication and cooperation than upon the way each decision was arrived at. However, when broad board policies are translated into specific meanings for internal application, the input and understandings of all directly involved should be solicited from time to time. Policies are not valid unless they are understandable and workable.

26. Making the tough decisions

When hard decisions such as confronting or dismissing personnel have to be made, the board's sense of Christian ethics, its social maturity, and its moral fiber (backbone) are put to severe tests.

Probably one of the weakest links in

the chain of decision making is indecision in dealing with personnel. Church organizations particularly tend under the guise of Christian love to overlook mediocre performance and inefficiency for too long and then act crudely, precipitously, and even deviously when finally prodded into action.

Good administration and good supervision will generally help improve weak performances. It is the duty of administration to evaluate performance, help upgrade where needed, and also be ready to commend when honest praise is deserved.

Some persons are miscast in the roles in which we have placed them and consequently may be incompetent in the assignment. The person who made the placement generally is responsible for directly or indirectly helping the person to improve or to recommend a separation. Removal from a job should never come as a great surprise, but rather as a final step after all remedial efforts have proved unsuccessful. Frankness and integrity characterize every step in the process.

It is extremely important to follow approved procedures and Christian guidelines in such cases because the best interests of the person involved, the institution, and the community must be served. Consider this approach:

(a) ANALYZE. Study the situation, get all possible facts, and have them properly at hand (written down with exact times and circumstances).

(b) ACCOST. The person confronted should know exactly what the problems are as seen by the board.

(c) ADVISE. Present carefully the options you wish to suggest.

(d) ANSWER. Be frank in answering questions; to bungle in this process leads to chaos.

(e) AFFIRM. Help individuals to see that you want to be helpful, that the present situation may call for a change but that this does not mean you would not support them for some other position more suited to their temperment and abilities.

(f) ABSORB. There is apt to be hostility. Accept this without too much defensiveness, knowing that the person before you may be in a state of trauma but if your action is reasonable, time will change present attitudes.

(g) ACT-AGREE. The process should be so carefully projected that all board members can come to a consensus on the matter and support the decision in the community.

(h) APPEASE. Seldom is anyone separated from a position without some dissension in the institution or the community. The best means of appeasement is for the board to establish the point that it carefully looked at the known facts and made an honest decision for the best interests of all concerned—part of the job for which it was elected.

40 (i) ACCOUNT. The board is ultimately

responsible. However, before critical matters reach the board, the administration should carefully go through the established procedures, unless the head administrator is the person directly involved.

(j) ADDENDUM. When serious confrontations are to be made, the matter may be brought to the attention of the person to be confronted through a carefully prepared written statement with a suggested time when the matter may be personally discussed. In this way the suggestions will have been carefully thought through and the person involved has a chance to analyze the suggestions carefully. The discussion can then be carried on in a more dispassionate environment.

There may be emergency situations, such as grossly immoral actions or irremediable ability to do the job, which would preclude some of the steps suggested above. However, even in highly emotional emergency situations we must be careful not to act precipitously. These suggestions are not made so that incompetent persons may continue in their positions but rather that justice prevails for all.

The person charged has the right to be heard personally, to know exactly what the charges are, to explain, to have peer surrogates speak on his or her behalf, to be given a chance to improve and to have adequate time before a new contract period to make amends.

41

IX.

The Minutes

27. Achieving a clear statement of the actions

Board minutes are extremely important. Official minutes should state exactly what happened. Boards should elect a secretary whose duty it is to analyze procedures, take notes, and record motions or understandings precisely as stated by the initiator of the action.

The exact wording of the action or motion should be read back before a decision is called for so that everyone understands what is being voted on. The minutes may be more valuable if in addition to motions or actions some descriptive or explanatory data is included. However, the real essence of the minutes is to provide a basic and clear statement of the actions.

The recording secretary puts the minutes into final shape. In some cases, administrators may be asked to have the copies of the minutes processed through their offices. The minutes at this state should be listed as "tentative minutes" and sent out to all board members for careful review before the next meeting.

Minutes should not be considered official until the members have read them, approved them, and accepted them through proper action at a regular board meeting. At this stage, in many organizations the president and secretary sign the minutes.

X.

Special Committees
28. Functions and limitations

Special committees including executive committees are at times appointed with power to act between regular meetings. However, if too many important decisions are made in this way the whole board can do no more than approve, reprimand, or rescind—all choices which are somewhat unpleasant. It is assumed that special committees should work closely with the administrator.

Capable administrators have learned the limits and responsibilities of delegated authority. The administrator is the person delegated to make the decisions between meetings within guidelines which should be carefully delineated unless the board has given a committee the power to act. If the administrator or a committee isn't sure, decisions should wait either for a regular board meeting or for a special meeting. If special meetings are impractical, an executive committee within reasonable geographical proximity should be empowered to act in given situations.

One item of business for the church board of trustees concerned a hole in the church roof. The action recorded: "A committee of three persons was appointed to look into the hole."

XI.

Executive Session
29. For board members only

There are times when it is advantageous for boards to meet in executive   43 session. This means that only elected or appointed persons are present. Generally, little official action should be taken during these sessions, but at times they may be necessary for matters which are entirely personal. Executive sessions will frequently center upon the administrator.

The board decides which private discussions should be brought to the attention of the administrator. If a regular time is arranged in the agenda for such sessions, however brief, it is accepted and understood as a regular occurrence and does not raise questions. Regular business should not be done at executive sessions to avoid public knowledge.

XII.

The Administrator—A Member of the Board?

30. A voting member

Generally, the chief executive or administrative officer of the board is not expected to be a voting member. However, there are some instances when boards include the administrator as a voting member. For example, the guidelines for Catholic hospital boards in St. Louis include the following: "The chief executive officer is the agent of the board. He acts as liaison between the board and the day-to-day hospital operation. He is responsible for implementing board policies and directives. Because of the importance of his position, it seems appropriate that he be a voting member of the board."[2]

Private boards can develop any procedures they wish, as long as they are not contrary to the common good. However, I do not feel that it is sound procedure for the administrator to be a voting member. Administrators should attend all board meetings excepting for executive sessions, but if they are members of the board in a legal sense, they enter into decisions affecting themselves as employees. If administrators were full members of the board, technically there could be no executive sessions because an executive session means that every official board member is present.

The board should be able to look at the administrator's recommendations and proposals entirely upon their merits. When voting administrators make proposals, it is assumed that they would vote for their recommendations; already the decision is tilted in the general direction of favoring the action. If administrators cannot make a good case for their recommendations by sound reasoning, they cannot do so effectively through an additional vote. In fact, such a vote might be divisive rather than helpful in moving forward to consensus. The administra-

---

2. *Guidelines on the Responsibilities, Functions, and Selection Criteria for Hospital Boards of Trustees* (St. Louis: Catholic Hospital Association), p. 20.

tor's duty is not that of legislation but bringing before the board recommendations which should be tested independently.

31. A member ex officio

An ex officio member of a board is by virtue of office a full-fledged voting member, and not just an honorary member as is often intended. There are some legitimate situations where this might be advisable. However, we should be careful not to confer this title on executive officers or advisory personnel.

XIII.

Consultants

32. Advice for special decisions

A board should realize that it has many resources beyond its administrator, its staff, and its own membership. In making certain decisions which are far from routine and when the consequences are especially significant, it is proper to secure counsel outside the immediate groups.

Frequently, there are persons in the church and community who have special skills and expertise which should be brought to bear on the problems at hand. It is a sign of strength rather than weakness for boards to know when broader information and technical skills are needed. The purpose of this method is not to shift responsibility but to make the best possible decisions.

XIV.

Authority Outside of Board Sessions

33. Adjourned is adjourned

One principle should be clearly kept in mind: No board member, including the chair, has any special authority when the board is not in session unless the whole body has previously delegated some special assignment to an individual or individuals.

"The board exists continously, but it acts only when in session. No individual member carries a responsibility in the board except as it is delegated to him by the entire body. However, the board carries constantly the responsibility for whatever goes on in the institution."[3]

34. Consultative role for the chairperson

It is quite natural that the chairperson might serve as a general counselor to the administrator, particularly if they reside in proximity to each other. However, the chairperson's role is only to counsel and should never become one of making decisions which will bind the whole board to some action which it may not freely have chosen to take. No person can know all the implications of any situation. No person can presume to know how a board will act as a body after each member has added personal knowledge and response.

If the president or other board person-

---

3. Paul Mininger, *Trustees are Directors* (Elkhart, Ind.: Mennonite Board of Missions, 1965), p. 3.

nel are expected to serve in special consultative roles with the administration, this can and should be spelled out by the board. One board's manual lists its chairperson's duties (here called president) as follows: "The president shall function as a counselor to the officers of the school."[4] This points up a consultative capacity which does not go into decision making.

XV.

Counseling the Administrator
35. Avoiding the lonelies"

Administrators live in a climate of loneliness. As representatives of the board to the staff they are apt to be thought of by staff as board members. When administrators bring the interests of the staff to the board, they may be thought of as staff. Administrators cannot become too intimate with any one group without raising questions on the part of others. It is difficult for the administrator to represent both camps effectively. Too often these groups are in separate camps. Their objectives may be parallel, but their specific interests are different.

The superintendent's son, a first-grader, said to his classmate, the principal's son, "My dad can fire your dad." "Yes, but good principals are hard to get," the other replied.

---

4. *Board Policies and Procedures Manual* (Goshen, Ind.: Bethany Christian High School), Code N. 6.331. This manual is properly updated each year. For outlining the duties and functions of the board and personnel, this manual is one of the best examples of clarity and completeness.

Board chairpersons should be instructed to keep close contact with the administrator. It is good if the two are close geographically so that the administrator, who has to make dozens of decisions between board meetings, can have the board chairperson as a resource. While board members, including the chairperson, do not have authority in and of themselves individually, the chairperson can give counsel when sought and be cognizant of the general welfare of the administrator. If close geographical contact is impossible, telephone calls can be helpful. Always, however, the prerogatives of administration and board responsibility must be carefully delineated and respected.

XVI.

Selecting an Administrator or Spiritual Leader

36. Takes time, effort, money

The best policies, programs, and procedures by boards cannot prevent the occasion wherein a new administrator or spiritual leader must be selected; good techniques will reduce the frequency of turnover, however.

The proper selection of an administrator or a spiritual leader is so important that a board must spend time, effort, and probably money in getting the right person. Sound procedures will pay big dividends in the long run. If you spend time wisely now it will save a lot of hard work later!

Generally it is best to declare openly that a vacancy exists. This is true even though a person within the organization may be strongly qualified and considered. Those within then know what is going on and have opportunity to express their opinions.

37. Important steps to follow

• Decide what your current and future leadership needs are and put them into writing. Careful writing will force you to be precise.

• Appoint a search committee made up of some board members and some persons from the constituency. The search committee should be broadly based sociologically. In a nonlocal constituency geographic representation is also important.

• The search committee should first hold a meeting to:

(a) Discuss qualifications and draw up a job description. Many of the qualifications for board members also apply to administrators.

(b) Scrutinize the candidate's spiritual qualifications carefully if yours is a religious organization. If it is not, keep in mind that the spiritual qualifications one would expect in a religious organization are often the same qualities which lead to success in secular fields.

(c) Determine the procedure for receiving applications.

(d) Set up the screening and interview process.

(e) Prepare pertinent information re- garding salary range.

(f) Establish a tentative time schedule.

• In inviting recommendations from without don't overlook those persons within the organization who have shown evidence of good growth and development. It is generally good for staff members to know that there is opportunity for promotion within.

• Don't overlook the fact that many women have good potential for positions which at one time were restricted to men, and vice versa.

• After the search committee compiles its list, it should screen carefully and select persons who seemingly have the proper credentials. However, before a potential prospect is contacted the present employer should be apprised and sanction such a contact.

• If the person contacted is interested in the position, his or her credentials are important. Some written materials on training, experience, and personal philosophy should be submitted. Examine the written credentials carefully. What is left out may be more important than what is said.

The following letter of recommendation was found in one man's credentials: "James Matthews worked for us for two years. He resigned. We are satisfied."

• The personal interview is very important. The candidate should come before the whole board and not the search committee. The search committee should make recommendations only. If the first candidate is not selected, 51 other recommendations should come from listings which the search committee has made.

In determining a list of qualifications for the job, you are suggesting the ideal person who does not exist. Be prepared to give up some expectations in exchange for others which are the most basic.

XVII.

The Executive Board

38. Facilitating the function of a large board

Some organizations or societies which have large boards, several dozen or more members, and do not meet at least monthly, find it necessary to delegate responsibilities through their bylaws to a small executive board. This body, geographically located to be able to get together rather easily, deals with probems which cannot wait for quarterly, semiannual, or annual meetings.

39. Limits are important

The duties of these smaller boards must be spelled out carefully since the power to act must be one of its functions. The officers of the total board should be part of the executive board if the total responsibility is to be well coordinated.

This arrangement, while necessary in some cases, has its hazards. Its function must be limited to certain specific well-defined actions because the total board is almost forced to ratify the executive board's past actions. This takes away some of the challenge and freedom from the official board of ultimate responsibility and may give its members a sense of being rubber stamps. The executive board is a solid and necessary option for doing business in some societies, however.

XVIII.

Conclusion

40. A case study for better management

J. Daniel Hess, professor of communication at Goshen College, Goshen, Indiana, in a paper, "The System's Approach to Personnel Management," made the following observations:

Is it not somewhat ironic that certain of our institutions perform a mission and please a customer and gain a good public image while leaving their own employees depressed?

In a widely respected business institution in which a department of employees seemed constantly troubled, I asked the employees to list what bothered them. The ten most frequently listed complaints were:

(a) We need a friendlier atmosphere, a place where "good mornings" and "how are things going?" are shared freely.

(b) My job could be improved if I did not have a dozen bosses.

(c) Could each employee's duties be more clearly defined? This would help me know the limits of my own responsibility and that of others.

(d) Our policies ought to be circulated, so there would not be partiality in administering them.

(e) The weekly newsletter is important. I consider it a courtesy to be told of new decisions before I read of them in the newspaper.

(f) Confidentiality in my superiors is important. If I feel he/she will spread around what I said in confidence, I will no longer speak freely.

(g) I wish I could erase the feeling that others think I am a flunkie, and my job a menial one.

(h) I've been around for quite a while. To this day, I have received no genuine compliment for my work.

(i) Friday is our busy day. Could we reopen the possibility of an hour lunch break and a brief midafternoon coffee?

(j) A woman here doesn't have much chance to climb the administrative ladder. How can we destroy the ceiling in our professional aspirations?

Notice that no mention was made of salaries, little or no mention was made about a distasteful task, little mention about working conditions. But involved in just about every complaint was an element of communication breakdown. Even an insignificant communication problem, we discovered at that institution, led to the deepest of frustrations.

41. How does your board measure up?

The ideas in this book speak to the following points. You may want to take stock of how your organization answers the challenge of creating boards that work.

Regarding your board:

(a) How is it selected? Are women and minorities considered?

(b) Does it have a good mix or cross section of members?

(c) What are the orientation procedures?

(d) What is its authority? Do your charter and bylaws outline this responsibility?

(e) How is the agenda made up?

(f) What is the source of the input?

(g) What is the process of decision making?

(h) How can members become better informed?

(i) What are you trying to do overall?

(j) What is the role of individual board members out of session?

(k) Do you have well-defined written policies and procedures?

(l) Are the minutes well kept? Where are they filed? To whom are they available?

(m) How are the board actions carried out?

(n) Who is accountable to whom throughout the organization?

(o) How are new members selected?

(p) What special criteria do you use in deciding whom you employ—Christian

"But all things should be done decently and in order" (1 Corinthians 14:40).

55

Notes standards, church membership, and so
forth?

(q) Is the delegation of authority well
defined?

(r) What are your procedures for review and appraisal?

(s) Do you provide for executive session?

(t) How _____ communicate your
plans, o_____ ___r
various
operatio

(u) B